Easy Picnic Cookbook

Delicious Easy Picnic Recipes for All Ages

Table of Contents

Introduction 4

    Potato Mini's 5

    Olives Green Bean Potato Salad 8

    Sugar Peas Mustard Seed Potato Salad 11

    Chicken BBQ Burger 13

    Creole Styled Meat–Free Burger 16

    Classic Veal Burgers 18

    Eggplant Parmesan Burgers 21

    Prosciutto, Cheese Olive Sandwiches 24

    Shrimp Burgers 26

    Italian Inspired Prosciutto Basil Panini 28

    Classy Garden Burger 30

    Montreal Tuna Burger 33

    Purple Potato Salad 36

    Pizza Burgers 38

    Quinoa Spring Vegetable Pilaf 41

    Philly Cheesesteak Burger 44

    Quinoa Tabbouleh 47

    Berry Peachy Turkey Burger 50

    Range Burger 53

    Radicchio Carrot Slaw 57

    Asian Chicken Burger 59

Introduction

Who doesn't love a good picnic?

Picnics are perfect for just about any occasion and what's even more perfect was that there are a variety of meals that would be perfect for the windy outdoors. Unfortunately, so many people seem to think that the only foods that can stand up to this unpredictable environment are sandwiches and though sandwiches were delicious you can enjoy so much more.

This Easy Picnic Cookbook will introduce you to so much more. From salads to spreads and to desserts. All enough for you to enjoy an elegant picnic with your guests that will leave just about everyone longing for more.

So, what are you waiting for? Flip the page to get started.

Roman BBQ Sliders 62

Radish, Chive Tea Sandwiches... 64

Radishes with Creamy Anchovy Butter............................. 66

Veggie Burger with Cheese 68

All–American Burger 71

Caribbean Chicken Burger 74

Blue Stuffed Burgers with Onion and Spinach 77

Juicy Lucy Burger 80

Blue Vidalia Burgers 83

Conclusion 86

Potato Mini's

Use baked waffle–cut potatoes in place on buns. This would be an excellent dish to serve to a small crowd as a little appetizer. Enlist some help and make a double batch.

Serves: 16

Time: 15 min

Ingredients:

- 16 Large Frozen Waffle–cut Potatoes
- 1 lb. Ground Beef
- 3 Tsp Your Favorite Grill Seasoning
- 4 Slices of Cheddar Cheese, Each Cut into 4 Pieces
- 4 Sliced Cherry Tomatoes
- Various Condiments (Ketchup, mustard, sour cream, pickles)

Directions:

1. Preheat oven to 400°F.

2. Line a baking sheet with foil and space the potatoes out on it. Bake until lightly browned and crispy (18 min).

3. While this is going, mix the meat and seasoning. Make 16 little mini burgers and fry them up on a med–high heat until internal temperature is 160°F (5 min). Turn once. Drain on kitchen paper towels.

4. Once the potatoes are done, set them aside and move the oven racks to roughly 5" from the element (don't forget to adjust the oven to broil to preheat).

5. Now grab one potato waffle thingy and top with a burger, a dinky little piece of cheese and a slice of tomato. Repeat x 16.

6. Broil briefly for a minute or two until it looks tasty.

7. Serve with your usual condiments like mustard and ketchup along with sour cream and pickles. Enjoy!

Olives Green Bean Potato Salad

This delicious potato salad is filled with vegetables and herbs to create a tasty warm salad.

Serves: 10

Time: 35 minutes

Ingredients:

- olive oil, 1/8 cup
- white wine vinegar, 1/4 cup
- shallots, 2 tbsps., minced
- anchovies, 4, minced

- parsley, 2 tsps., chopped
- basil, 2 tsps., chopped
- marjoram, 2 tsps., chopped
- green beans, 8 oz., trimmed
- wax beans, 8 oz., yellow, trimmed
- Yukon Gold potatoes, 2 lbs., unpeeled, cubed
- red onion, 1/2 cup, chopped
- green olives, 1/2 cup, pitted, halved
- Niçois olives, 1/2 cup, pitted, halved
- Capers, 1/4 cup, drained

Directions:

1. Mix olive oil, vinegar, shallots and anchovies in medium bowl.

2. Whisk in about a teaspoon each of basil, parsley and marjoram. Season with pepper and salt to taste.

3. Set a saucepan on high heat with water to boil then add in all your beans to cook for about 5 minutes or until tender yet crisp.

4. Drain and light rinse beneath cold water then dry with a napkin.

5. Cover separately, then place to refrigerate. Leave to stand at room temperature for about 2 hours.

6. Allow the potatoes to steam for about 12 minutes or until just about tender.

7. Place your potatoes into a large bowl then set your dressing to warm up in the microwave for about 30 seconds. Add the dressing over the potatoes then toss to coat.

8. Transfer your potatoes to the center of the platter to create a small mound then combine your remaining dressing beans in a bowl.

9. Add in your beans around your potatoes. Sprinkle with onion, olives, capers and herbs. Serve warm or at room temperature.

Sugar Peas Mustard Seed Potato Salad

A simple salad with a tangy dressing-perfect for and April picnic.

Serves: 4

Time: 25 minutes

Ingredients:

- olive oil, 1/3 cup
- Dijon mustard, whole grain, 5 tbsps.
- mustard seeds, yellow, 3 tbsps.

- Dill, 3 tbsp., chopped
- white wine vinegar, 2 tbsp.
- red-skinned potatoes, 1 1/2 lbs., medium, cut into wedges then halved
- sugar snap peas, 8 oz., stringed
- red onion, 1/2 cup, chopped

Directions:

1. Blend your first 5 ingredients in a bowl then season with pepper and salt.

2. Set your potatoes to steam for about 10 minutes or until just tender. Once cooked transfer your potatoes to a bowl then lightly coat with 3 tablespoons.

3. Set your snap peas to steam for 2 minutes, or until tender yet crisp. Set to cool. Add to bowl with potatoes.

4. Add red onion and remaining dressing then toss to coat and season to taste with pepper and salt.

5. Enjoy

Chicken BBQ Burger

Use minced chicken and corn instead of beef. This recipe uses and extra bun for making bread crumbs; so, if you have some ready–made stuff on hand you would rather use, you only need 6 buns.

Serves: 6

Time: 5 mins

Ingredients

The Burger:

- 1 Small Chopped Onion (1 cup)
- 1 Tsp Your Vegetable Oil of Choice
- 6 (+1 Extra) Round Buns (+1 Extra bun for the food processor)
- 1 lb. Ground Chicken
- 1 Egg, Lightly Beaten
- 3 Tbsp Your Favorite Barbecue Sauce
- ½ Tsp Salt
- ¼ Tsp Ground Black Pepper
- 1 cup Corn Kernels (Fresh or thawed from frozen)

To Serve:

- Sliced Red Onion, enough for topping
- Barbecue Sauce, as preferred

Directions

1. Heat your oven broiler and give the rack a poof or two of cooking spray

2. Sauté onion on med–low until softened (10 min) but don't let them brown.

3. While the onions are sweating away, savagely rip a bun apart and pop into a food processor. Pulse until there is nothing left but fine crumbs.

4. Mix the ground chicken, lightly beaten egg, and the rest of the burger ingredients together. Shape into 6 balls and then pat them into, well, patties.

5. Grill or broil roughly 4″ from the heat. Turn after about 5 min. and cook until done (165°F), which will take another 5 min or so.

6. Serve with the rolls, garnishing with onion slices and extra sauce and any of your favorite trimmings.

7. Enjoy!

Creole Styled Meat-Free Burger

Grab a known carnivore and have them see what they think of this one

Serves: 4

Time: 15 min

Ingredients

Patties:

- 1 x Can (15 oz) Red Kidney Beans: Rinsed and Mashed
- 1 Onion, Sliced
- 1 Egg (Raw, for binding)

- 1 Tbsp Tomato Sauce/Ketchup
- 1 Tsp Mustard (Pre–made)
- 2 Tsp Worcestershire Sauce
- ¼ Tsp Cumin (Ground)
- 3 Tbsp Bread Crumbs (Flavored ones can be used)
- To Serve:
- 1 Tbsp Vegetable Oil (For frying)
- 4 x Buns
- Lettuce
- Thousand Island Salad Dressing, to taste

Directions

1. Mix all the ingredients and form into 4 patties.

2. Heat oil in a pan over a med–low heat.

3. Fry for 3 minutes on each side.

4. Serve with buns and lettuce with dressing.

Classic Veal Burgers

If you like the taste of game meat, this one is for you: good spices, rye bread and swiss cheese

Serves: 4

Time: 20 min

Ingredients

Burger:

- 1 Egg, Lightly Beaten with a Fork
- 2 Tbsp Water (or Beer, if you happen to have some)
- 1 Slice Rye Bread Turned into Crumbs (¾ cup)
- ½ Tsp Caraway Seeds
- ½ Tsp Dried Marjoram
- 1 Clove Garlic, Finely Sliced
- ¼ Tsp Salt
- ¼ Tsp Black Pepper
- 1 lb. Ground Beef

To Serve:

- 8 Slices of Rye Bread (9 slices in total, one was for making crumbs)
- 4 x 1 oz Slices Swiss Cheese
- 3 Tbsp Mustard of Choice

Directions

1. Get your grill to a good medium heat.

2. Stir together the egg and water/beer, then add the crumbs, caraway, marjoram, garlic, and seasoning. Now mix the meat in well and shape into four patties: ¾" thick.

3. Pop the patties on an oiled grill rack, directly over the heat. Grill (uncovered) until the internal temp is 160°F (16–18 min) turning once halfway.

4. Just before you remove the burgers, add the bread to the grill and toast one side lightly (1–2 min). Turn them, put a slice of cheese on four of them and toast the bottoms (1–2 min).

5. Serve the cheese–topped bread with the patties on top. Then spread the un–cheesed ones with mustard and close the burger.

Eggplant Parmesan Burgers

Not everyone appreciates a good eggplant. Try this recipe on them see if you can change their minds.

Serves: 2

Time: 15 min

Ingredients

Eggplant:

- ½ Tsp Oil
- 1 Egg White, Stirred in a Little Dish
- ½ cup Panko Bread Crumbs

- 1 Tbsp 1 Tbsp of Grated Parmesan Cheese (2 in total)
- ¼ Tsp Pepper
- ¼ Tsp Dried Parsley
- 4 x ½–" Thick Slices of Eggplant (Peeled)

Patties:

- 8 oz Ground Beef
- A Dash of Garlic Powder
- Yet Another Egg White
- ½ cup Marinara Sauce, Warmed Up
- 1 oz Grated Mozzarella Cheese (¼ cup)
- 1 cup Arugula Leaves (aka Rocket)

Directions

1. Bring your charcoal/gas grill to medium hot.

2. Preheat oven to 375°F grease an oven–proof dish/baking sheet with oil.

3. Grab a shallow bowl mix a ⅓ cup of the panko, 1 Tbsp of the Parmesan, a dash of black pepper, the parsley flakes.

4. Dip each eggplant slice in the egg white first then into the crumb mixture, then onto the prepared dish/sheet. Lightly spray some cooking spray over the lot.

5. Bake until golden crispy, turning them once (30 min)

6. While the eggplant is crisping cooking, mix the meat up with remaining panko, the second tablespoon of Parmesan the second egg white. Add a dash of pepper the garlic powder.

7. Divide this mix up into 4 patties: ½″ thick

8. Pop them onto the grill, directly above the heat, cover grill until internal temp is 160°F, turning once (8–10 min).

9. Top each golden slice of eggplant with a patty some marinara sauce. Sprinkle mozzarella over each one top with arugula.

Prosciutto, Cheese Olive Sandwiches

These elevated sandwiches are easy to make and delicious.

Serves: 6

Time: 30 minutes

Ingredients:

- 1 large plum tomato, seeded and chopped
- 3 tablespoons black olive paste
- 1/4 cup chopped fresh basil leaves
- 1 lb., fresh mozzarella, sliced

- 4 cups trimmed arugula, chopped coarsely
- 2 tablespoons extra-virgin olive oil
- 1 Parmesan Focaccia, halved horizontally
- 1/2 pound thinly sliced prosciutto

Directions:

1. In a bowl stir together basil, olive paste and tomato.

2. Add mozzarella and arugula in another bowl then toss with pepper, salt and oil to taste.

3. Spread your olive mixture on top of the focaccia. Top olive mixture with arugula, prosciutto, mozzarella and remaining focaccia half.

4. Apply light pressure then slice lengthwise in half, then again crosswise to create 6 small sandwiches.

5. Cut sandwiches diagonally in half and wrap tightly in plastic wrap.

6. Chill sandwiches at least 1 hour and up to 1 day. Enjoy!

Shrimp Burgers

Here we have a seafood take on a hamburger. Simple tasty.

Serves: 4

Time: 10 min

Ingredients:

- Round Rolls, 2, processed into Crumbs
- Shrimp, 1¼ lb., deveined, finely chopped
- Mayo, ⅓ cup

- Salt, 1 tsp.
- Pepper, ½ tsp.
- Butter, 2 tbsp.
- For Serving:
- Hamburger Rolls, 4
- Iceberg Lettuce, 6 leaves
- Tartar Sauce, enough to cover rolls

Directions:

1. Add shrimp to crumbs then add seasoning and mayo. Toss to combine.

2. Carefully form the mixture into 4 patties.

3. Set your non-stick skillet on medium heat with enough butter to grease and cook the patties until cooked through, flipping halfway (about 9 mins).

4. Serve on the cut open buns with lettuce tartar sauce.

Italian Inspired Prosciutto Basil Panini

This Italian inspired sandwich is a picnic dream.

Serves: 4

Time: 20 minutes

Ingredients:

- olive oil, 1/2 cup
- balsamic vinegar, 3 tbsp.

- garlic, 1 clove, minced
- prosciutto, 8 oz., thinly sliced
- mozzarella cheese, 10 oz., thinly sliced
- tomato, 12 slices
- basil, 12 large leaves
- ciabatta bread, 16oz., halved horizontally

Directions:

1. Whisk garlic, vinegar and olive oil in small bowl to blend; use salt and pepper to season dressing to taste.

2. Layer basil, tomato, mozzarella and prosciutto over bottom of bread.

3. Drizzle the dressing lightly on the sandwich and season once more with salt and pepper. Top with the remaining slice of bread then slice into 4 quarters.

4. Preheat your barbecue to medium heat. Set the sandwiches to grill for about 5 minutes on each side or until beautifully golden brown with melted cheese. Press occasionally with a large spatula to compact.

5. Enjoy!

Classy Garden Burger

Cook these on an open fire for a full smoky flavor. Notes of freshly ground black pepper fresh thyme. Top with blue cheese, rocket, summer squash, red onion pickles.

Serves: 4

Time: 20 mins

Ingredients:

Dressing:

- 2 Tbsp Oil
- 2 Tbsp Wine Vinegar (Red)
- 1 Tsp Freshly Chopped Thyme
- ¼ Tsp Coarsely Ground Black Pepper

Burger:

- 1 lb. Ground Beef
- ¼ Tsp Salt
- ¼ Tsp Pepper

Toppings:

- 2 Med–sized Summer Squashes, sliced lengthways
- 2–4 oz Blue Cheese Wedges
- Arugula, as much as you please

To Serve:

- 4 Round Buns, Opened Toasted
- Tomato Slices
- Red Onion Slices

- Pickle Slices

Directions

1. Mix the oil, vinegar, thyme pepper together. You could throw it together in a sealable bottle shake while singing "If you are happy you know it". If you are feeling more serious, just mix with a teaspoon.

2. Grab a big bowl mix the meat, ¼ Tsp salt ¼ Tsp pepper. Make four equal balls of this mix compress them to form ¼" patties.

3. Brush the squash with some of the dressing set aside

4. Preheat, reduce to med–hot grill as above (cook covered).

5. Pop the meat into the buns drizzle some dressing over the cut face of the top half of the bun.

6. Top with the topping things serve.

Montreal Tuna Burger

Here is another take on the steak au poivre, merely a fancy term for "pepper steak"

Serves: 6

Time: 15 min

Ingredients

- ½ cup Sour Cream
- 2 Tbsp Chopped Parsley
- 2 Tsp Chopped Shallots

- 1 Tsp Honey Dijon Mustard
- 6 x 4 oz Tuna Steaks (1″ Thick)
- 6 Large Slices Sourdough Bread Cut in Half Crosswise
- 2 Tsp Montreal Steak Seasoning
- 1 Small Bunch of Chicory/Endive Leaves

Directions

1. Get whichever grilling method you prefer to a good medium–heat. Oil or spray the rack you will be using.

2. Combine the sour cream, parsley, chopped shallots and honey mustard. Cover and keep in the fridge until serving time – which is only one paragraph away.

3. Use your Montreal seasoning on both sides of your tuna. Grill for 6 minutes in total, turning once. Keep the cooked tuna warm on a plate.

4. Spread the cream mix onto the top portions of the buns, then lay the tuna and endives inside before closing and serving.

5. Use 2 tsp. of your sour cream mixture to spread on each bread slice.

6. Top a half of your bread halves with a tuna steak then Frisee. Top with your other bread halves and serve.

7. Enjoy!

Purple Potato Salad

This recipe was created to accompany Seared Rosemary Scallops.

Serves: 2

Time: 45 minutes

Ingredients:

- 1/2 pound small purple potatoes, quartered
- 1/4 pound sugar snap peas, trimmed

- 2 tsp. balsamic vinegar
- 2 tsp. extra-virgin olive oil
- 10 fresh mint leaves, sliced thin

Directions:

1. Allow your potatoes to cook in a saucepan covered with cold salted water for about 20 minutes or until tender.

2. Transfer your cooked potatoes into a colander to drain. Set to cool for about 10 minutes.

3. Next, set your snap peas to blanch for about a minute, until tender yet crisp.

4. Drain the peas quickly then run under cold water. Drain once more then pat dry.

5. In a bowl toss together potatoes, snap peas, vinegar, oil, mint, and salt and pepper to taste.

6. Place to chill or enjoy!

Pizza Burgers

Ah, finally, you no longer have to choose which one you want… two for the price of one!

Serves: 4

Time 20 min

Ingredients:

Burger Mix:

- 1 Egg, Lightly Beaten with a Fork
- ⅓ cup Canned Mushrooms, Drained Sliced
- ¼ cup Seasoned Bread Crumbs
- 2 Tbsp Milk
- 1 Tsp Dried Italian Herb Mix
- ¼ Tsp Salt

Sauce:

- 1 Can Pizza Sauce (8 oz)
- ¼ cup Sliced Olives
- 1 lb. Ground Pork

To Serve:

- 8 Man–sized Chunks of French Bread
- ¼ cup Mozzarella Cheese Grated (1 oz)

Directions:

1. Build your charcoal grill get the coals to a med–high heat.

2. For gas, preheat at full blast then set the temp to med–hot. Cover grill as for charcoal.

3. Combine the beaten egg, mushrooms, bread crumbs, milk, seasoning, salt. Mix in the meat shape into four patties, ¾" thick.

4. Grill until internal temp is 160°F (14–18 min), turning once at the halfway point. Toast the bread in the last few minutes of cooking the meat.

5. Put the olives pizza sauce in a little pot cook until the olives are heated through.

6. Serve burgers between slices of bread with the pizza olive sauce sprinkle with a bit of cheese.

Quinoa Spring Vegetable Pilaf

For a hardier picnic meal try this delicious quinoa pilaf.

Serves: 4

Time: 1 hour

Ingredients:

- quinoa, 1 1/2 cups, well rinsed
- vegetable broth, 1 cup
- petite peas, 2 cups, frozen, thawed
- mint leaves, 5 tbsp. chopped, divided
- garlic, 1 clove, peeled

- butter, 3 tbsp.
- leek, 1 cup, thinly sliced
- shallots, 3/4 cup, sliced
- shiitake mushrooms, 8 oz., stemmed, thickly sliced
- asparagus, 14 oz., trimmed, sliced diagonal into 1-inch pieces

Directions:

1. Set your quinoa to cook in 2 1/2 cups of boiling water with a tsp of salt. Start on high then reduce the heat to a simmer then cover and cook for about 17 minutes or until all the water has been absorbed. Drain, if needed.

2. Puree broth, garlic, 4 tbsp mint and 1 cup peas in blender until smooth.

3. Melt butter in large nonstick skillet over medium heat. Add in your shallots and leek then sauté for about 4 minutes, until light brown and soft.

4. Stir in asparagus then mushrooms; sauté until your mushrooms become tender and the asparagus are tender, yet crisp, maybe about 5 minutes.

5. Add in a cup of your peas and puree; stir for about 2 minutes or until heated through. Add in quinoa then lightly stir.

6. Separate into serving bowls; sprinkle with remaining 1 tablespoon mint and serve.

7. Enjoy.

Philly Cheesesteak Burger

The burger version of this famous steak. The topping includes fried mushroom, sweet peppers, and onions.

Serves: 6

Time: 15 min

Ingredients

Burger Patties:

- 1½ lb. Ground Beef Sirloin

Toppings:

- 1 Tbsp Oil – Olive or Canola
- 1 Large Onion
- 1 Sweet Red Pepper, Insides Removed and Sliced Up
- ½ lb. Button Mushrooms, Sliced

To Serve:

- 12 Thin Slices of Cheese, Preferably Provolone (±6 oz)
- Pepperoncini (For garnish)
- ¾ lb. Hamburger Buns

Directions

1. Get the coals going. You want med–hot coals or a med–hot gas grill (preheat on high and then drop the temp to med–hot). Grease the rack you plan to use.

2. Form the meat into six patties and pop in the fridge for later.

3. Now prepare the topping:

4. Fry the onions alone in 1 Tbsp of oil for around 5 min over a med–hot stove. Then add the peppers and mushrooms and cook until tender (4–5 min).

5. Cover (if using a gas grill) and grill until the internal temp is 160°F (6 min). Turn off heat and quickly place 2 slices of cheese on the top of each one. Wait until the cheese melts before serving.

6. Put each burger in a hamburger bun and spoon the topping over it.

7. Serve with pepperoncini and enjoy.

Quinoa Tabbouleh

The classic Middle Eastern salad proves to be a delicious vegetarian main course and a summer-suitable side.

Serves: 6

Time: 25 minutes

Ingredients:

- 1 cup quinoa, rinsed well
- 1/2 tsp. kosher salt (maybe more based on taste)

- 2 tablespoon fresh lemon juice
- 1 garlic clove, minced
- 1/2 cup extra-virgin olive oil
- Freshly ground black pepper
- Cucumber, 1, English hothouse
- 1 pint cherry tomatoes, halved
- 2/3 cup chopped flat-leaf parsley
- 1/2 cup chopped fresh mint
- 2 scallions, thinly sliced

Directions:

1. Allow quinoa to cook in 1 1/4 cups water with salt. Allow to boil over the high heat then reduce the heat to low, cover, then simmer for about 10 minutes or until quinoa is tender.

2. Switch off the heat then allow to stand, covered, for 5 minutes. Fluff with a fork.

3. Meanwhile, whisk your garlic and lemon juice in a small bowl. Then whisk in your olive oil gradually. Season with pepper and salt to taste.

4. Transfer your quinoa to a large rimmed baking sheet, spread into a thin sheet then let cool. Transfer to a large bowl; mix in 1/4 cup dressing.

5. Add scallions, herbs, tomatoes and cucumber to bowl with quinoa; toss to coat. Season to taste with salt and pepper.

6. Drizzle remaining dressing over. Enjoy!

Berry Peachy Turkey Burger

This is the epitome of creative. Give this show–stopper a try!

Serves: 4

Time: 30 min

Ingredients

Burger:

- 1 lb. Ground Turkey
- Salt and Pepper

- 4 Slices of Cheese (Monterey jack)
- 4 Peaches

Peach Mix:

- ½ cup of Fresh Blueberries
- ¼ Tsp Chili Powder
- 4 large slices of Garlic Bread
- Freshly Plucked Mint Leaves

Directions

1. Take one peach and chop it into tiny, little bits.

2. Then mix it together with the turkey and seasoning. You are now ready to shape into patties: 4 x ½" thick.

3. Set your grill to med–high and pop the patties onto a rack directly over the heat. Cook until there is no pink sections left inside; internal temp 165°F (roughly 5 min/side).

4. While you wait for the meat to cook, locate the other three peaches and chop them coarsely (but neatly). Get the blueberries, chili powder and peaches cooking on medium until they are nicely warmed; this will be just as the juices start to appear (5 min).

5. When the patties are ready, put the cheese on top, cover and cook on the grill again until it has melted just a bit (1 min).

6. Assembling:

1st Layer: Garlic bread

2nd Layer: Turkey burger with melted cheese

3rd Layer: Chili–peach mix

4th Layer: A little mint leaf or two

Final Layer: If you like, sprinkle a light dusting of chili powder over the lot to garnish.

7. Enjoy!

Range Burger

Here is a recipe with a bit of zing to it. It has apples, bison, cantaloupes, strawberries, cayenne pepper and citrus zest among other amazing ingredient combos.

Serves: 6

Time: 30 mins.

Ingredients

Apple Mix:

- Granny Smith Apple, finely chopped (½ cup)
- Stalk of Celery, finely sliced (⅓ cup)
- Onion, finely sliced (⅓ cup)

- 1 Tbsp Olive Oil

Burgers:

- 3 Tbsp Ketchup
- 1 Tsp Jerk Seasoning
- ¼ Tsp Salt
- ¼ Tsp Ground Black Pepper or Cayenne Pepper
- 1½ lb. Uncooked Ground Bison or Lean Ground Beef

To Serve:

- 6 Man–sized Slices of Rustic Bread
- ¼ cup Melted Butter
- Red–tipped Leaf Lettuce

Melon Relish:

- Orange–fleshed Melon: Flesh, chopped (1 cup)
- Strawberries, chopped (1 cup)
- Red Onion, finely chopped (¼ cup)
- Sweet Green Pepper, finely chopped (¼ cup)
- Cilantro, 2 tbsp., freshly chopped
- Mint Leaves, 1 tbsp., freshly snipped

- Lemon or Lime Zest, 1 tsp.
- Lemon or Lime Juice, 2 tbsp.

Directions

1. Fry apple, celery and onion in hot oil over med–heat until mixture is tender (6–8 min); then leave it to cool down to room temperature.

2. Grab a large bowl and pop the apple mixture, ketchup, and all the seasoning. Add the meat (bison/beef) and mix well. Divide into six ¾" thick burger patties.

3. Charcoal: Grill patties on a well–oiled rack of an open grill directly over med–hot coals until no longer pink; internal temp 160°F (16–18 min). Turning once, halfway.

4. Gas grill: Preheat and drop the heat to med–hot. Grill as above.

5. Just before removing the meat, toast the bread on both sides. Brush with melted butter when you're done.

6. Top the toast with lettuce, patties and melon relish.

7. Combine the chopped melon, strawberries, onion, sweet pepper, cilantro, fresh mint, lemon/lime zest and juice. Toss lightly to coat everything in the juice.

8. Leave it to sit at room temperature for half an hour or so, stirring now and then. This way the flavors will combine. Enjoy!

Radicchio Carrot Slaw

This slaw is wonderfully delicious yet classic.

Serves: 8

Time: 30 minutes

Ingredients:

- radicchio, 2 heads, halved and sliced thinly
- mayonnaise, 2/3 cup
- sugar, 2 tbsp.
- fennel seed, 1 tsp., dried
- carrots, 3/4 cup, roughly grated

- white wine vinegar, 1/3 cup
- Salt and pepper

Directions:

1. In a large mixing bowl, toss all the ingredients together.

2. Serve chilled.

Asian Chicken Burger

The chicken is not from Asia. But the concept is!

Serves: 4

Time: 15 mins

Ingredients

- 6 Finely Sliced Scallions (Include some of the green)
- 1 x Drained 8 oz Can of Water Chestnuts, Chopped
- ½ cup Sweet and Sour Duck Sauce (Orange sauce)
- 2 Tbsp Oil of Choice

- 2 oz Shiitake Mushrooms, Chopped
- 1 Clove Garlic, Finely Chopped
- 1 lb. Ground Chicken
- 2 Tbsp Freshly Chopped Cilantro
- 1 Tbsp Soy Sauce
- ¼ Tsp Salt
- A Dash of Black Pepper
- 4 Sesame Seed Round Buns, Best Served Warm

Directions

1. Mix roughly 2 Tbsp of the sliced scallions with an equal amount of chopped chestnuts and duck sauce.

2. Fry up the mushrooms, remaining scallions and garlic until they look tender (3 min). Leave it to cool a little and then add the mushroom mix with the chicken, remaining chestnut, cilantro and soy sauce in a bowl

3. Make up four patties about ¾" thick. Season the tops of the patties with a little salt and pepper.

4. Fry the patties in the recently abandoned pan (salted side down); med–heat. Sprinkle some more salt and pepper on them. Cook until 165°F (16–18 min), gently turning once.

5. Pop a burger in each warmed bun, garnish with a cilantro sprig and a side of sauce. Enjoy!

Roman BBQ Sliders

A slider is typically a small burger. This is ideal for a cocktail party.

Serves: 12

Time: 15 min

Ingredients:

- 3 lbs. Ground Beef
- ¼ cup Your Favorite Steak Sauce
- Salt Pepper

- 1 Bag Roma Tomatoes
- 1 Bunch Fresh Basil
- 24 Round Rolls
- Pesto Mayo Sauce (Mix ½ cup mayo with 2 Tbsp of basil pesto)
- Fresh Mozzarella Cheese, As Needed

Directions:

1. Get your gas/charcoal fire to medium heat.

2. Grab a large bowl add the meat, sauce seasoning. Mix well. Shape the meat into 24 patties.

3. Brush the grill with oil pop the burgers on. Cook for 4–6 min/side, depending on how well you want them done.

4. Halve the buns toast the cut side on the grill.

5. Spread pesto mayo on both sides of each bun pop the patties in with a slice of cheese, tomato a fresh leaf of basil.

6. Enjoy!

Radish, Chive Tea Sandwiches

These delicious sandwiches can be whipped up in minutes and are extremely tasty.

Serves: 16

Time: 30 minutes

Ingredients:

- butter, 4 tbsp., room temperature
- chives, 3 tbsp., minced, divided

- sesame seeds, 1 tbsp., toasted
- ginger, 3/4 tsp., grated, peeled
- Asian sesame oil, 1/4 tsp.
- Baguette, 16 slices
- radishes, 10, thinly sliced
- Fleur de sel (optional)*

Directions:

1. Mix oil, ginger, sesame seeds, butter and 2 tablespoons chives in small bowl; season with pepper and salt.

2. Spread your baguette with butter mixture. Top with radishes, overlapping slightly.

3. Sprinkle with fleur de sel and remaining chives, if desired. Enjoy.

Radishes with Creamy Anchovy Butter

This delicious French inspired canape is very simple yet delicious.

Serves: 8

Time: 40 minutes

Ingredients:

- butter, 1 1/2 sticks, unsalted, softened
- anchovy paste, 2 tbsp.

- garlic, 1 clove, chopped
- lemon juice, 1/4 tsp or to taste
- radishes, 24 small, halved

Directions:

1. Add your butter with lemon juice, garlic and anchovy paste then blend until smooth. Season with salt.

2. Serve as a dip for radishes.

Veggie Burger with Cheese

This is a tasty meat–alternative burger and is fairly low in glycemic load. Fry these up in your kitchen, but you could also do them on the grill outside.

Serves: 4

Time: 20 mins

Ingredients:

Patties:

- Chickpeas, canned, 2 cups, drained
- Onion, 1 Medium, cut into wedges
- Oats, ½ cup
- Chili Powder, 1 tbsp.
- Salt, 1 dash
- Black pepper
- Swiss Cheese, 1 cup, grated

Extras:

- Liquid from Peas, As Needed
- Oil, 1 Tbsp.
- Your preferred toppings

Directions

1. Get the patty ingredients together (peas, onions, oats, chili powder, salt, pepper, and cheese) in a food processor and pulse lightly until chunky (mash, not mush).

2. If it seems a little on the dry side, add some of the liquid from the bean can little bit by little. You want moist, not wet concoction going there.

3. Let the mix sit in the fridge or for a bit until it is firm enough to handle. Then make your four patties and put it back in the fridge for as long as you can (20 min if possible).

4. Heat your pan on med–high and coat with oil. Fry the patties until brown (10 min) – turning only once.

5. Serve on hamburger rolls with your favorite toppings. Enjoy!

All-American Burger

It's a well, burger. But not just any ole' burger... This one will be your go-to recipe when you need something a bit more interesting than a plain patty on a bun.

Serves: 4

Time: 25 min

Ingredients

Relish:

- ½ cup Roasted Red Pepper, Sliced
- 1 Tbsp Finely Chopped Olives
- 2 Tsp Oil

- 2 Tsp Freshly Snipped Thyme (or ½ Tsp dried)
- ¼ Tsp Black Pepper

Burger:

- ¼ cup Finely Chopped Onion
- 2 Tbsp Bread Crumbs
- 2 Tbsp Ketchup
- 1 Tbsp Horseradish Paste
- 1 Tbsp Mustard
- ¼ Tsp Salt
- ¼ Tsp Pepper
- 1 lb. Ground Beef
- 4 Slices Smoked Mozzarella Cheese

To Serve:

- 4 Hamburger Buns, Cut Open and Toasted Lightly
- Fresh Basil Leaves

Directions

1. Get your grill (gas or charcoal) to a good medium heat. The coals will be ready when they have a layer of gray ash on them.

2. Pop the pepper strips, olives, oil, thyme, and ¼ Tsp of black pepper into a food processor, mix a little before pulsing. You want the food chopped, not liquidized, so be careful. Cover this and leave it to chill in the fried until serving time.

3. Mix up the onions bread crumbs, ketchup, horseradish, mustard, salt, and the second ¼ Tsp pepper in a bowl. Add the meat and mix until just combined. Divide this mix into 4 patties that are roughly ¾" thick

4. Pop the patties onto an oiled grill rack and cook until the internal temp is 160°F (16–18 min). Remember to turn only once halfway through cooking. Just before you take the meat off, lay a slice of cheese on the top of each one so that it can melt a bit.

5. Serve on a toasted bun with fresh basil and 1 Tbsp of per bun of red sweet pepper relish.

Caribbean Chicken Burger

An interesting mix of flavors guaranteed to inspire you

Serves: 4

Time: 20 min

Ingredients

Burgers:

- 2 Slices of Bread, ripped into chunks
- 1 lb. Ground Chicken
- ½ cup Whole Milk
- 1 Tsp Onion Powder or Onion Soup Powder

- 1 Tsp Salt
- ¼ Tsp Thyme
- 8 Slices Sourdough Bread
- ½ Tsp Allspice (Nutmeg, cinnamon and clove in equal quantities)

Mango Relish:

- 2 Tbsp Finely Chopped Onion
- 1 Tbsp Wine Vinegar (Red)
- 1 Tsp Sugar
- Pinch of Salt
- 1 Medium–sized Mango, Flesh Diced (1 cup)
- 1 Tbsp Freshly Chopped Cilantro

Directions

1. Get the grill/or coals to a good medium heat.

2. Make fresh breadcrumbs by pulsing the bread bits in a food processor and keep aside for a minute. Now to pulse the patty ingredients (ground chicken, whole milk, onion powder, salt, and spices) until just combined, then add the crumbs you just made. Shape into 4 neat patties.

3. To make the relish, you will need a microwavable bowl to mix together the onion, vinegar, sugar, and salt. Nuke on high for a minute and leave it to cool for at least 30 sec.

4. Once, cooled a little, stir in the mango bits and chopped cilantro.

5. Brush the patties with oil or coat with cooking spray. Grill for 8 min, turning only once. It should be cooked through.

6. Just before the cooking time is up, grill the bread.

7. Serve everything together with the tasty relish.

Blue Stuffed Burgers with Onion and Spinach

If you like blue cheese, this one if for you. If not, feel free to substitute the blue for your favorite variety.

Serves: 4

Time: 25 mins

Ingredients

Burgers:

- 1 lb. Ground Beef
- 1 Tbsp Worcestershire Sauce
- 1 Tsp Black Pepper
- ½ cup Crumbled Blue Cheese

Trimmings:

- 1 Med-size Onion, Sliced Thinly
- A Splash or Two of Olive Oil for Brushing
- Salt to Taste

To Serve:

- 4 Hamburger Buns, Cut Open
- 1 cup Baby Spinach Leaves

Directions

1. Get your grill ready to go at a medium heat – no need to preheat because you will be cooking the meat uncovered. This would apply to a charcoal grill as well.

2. Mix the meat, Worcestershire sauce, and pepper in a large bowl.

3. Divide the mix into 8 balls. Pat them out until they are nice and thin: 4" in diameter. Half of these are tops, the other half tails.

4. Put 1 Tbsp of cheese on 4 of the patties. Toss a coin to see which side will get it, then match it with its mate and pinch the edges to seal it.

5. Brush onion rings with oil and scatter salt on them.

6. Grill burgers and onions on an oiled rack, directly over med–high heat. Grill until done: internal temp of 160°–165°F (5 min).

7. Brush the cut faces of the buns with oil and toast them in the last few moments of grilling the meat.

8. Serve on hamburger buns with the onion, spinach, and any remaining cheese.

Juicy Lucy Burger

A Juicy Lucy burger (traditionally) is a burger stuffed with cheese. Make sure that it has cooled somewhat before attempting to bite it. The cheese and steam may burn you.

Serves: 6

Time: 35 mins.

Ingredients

Burger Patty:

- 1 cup of Breadcrumbs
- ½ cup of Whole Milk (or Beef broth for a tasty, dairy–free option)
- 1 Egg
- ¼ cup Seasoned Bread Crumbs
- 2 Tbsp Worcestershire Sauce
- ¾ Tsp Salt
- ½ Tsp Freshly Ground Black Pepper
- 2 lbs. Ground Beef
- 12 x ¾ oz Slices of Cheese (American or swiss) Cut into 4 Pieces

To Serve:

- 6 Large Hamburger Buns
- Your favorite condiments (Pickles//ketchup/tomatoes/relish)

Directions

1. Soak the soft bread crumbs in milk for a few minutes before adding in the egg and dry crumbs along with

Worcestershire sauce and seasoning. Now add the meat and mix very gently.

2. Divide the mix into 12 balls and pat half of them down to roughly ½" thick and 3½" wide. These are the "lids". The remaining six will form the "pots" that you will pop your cheese into: just push a depression into the ball with the bottom of a drinking glass. Fill and seal the whole lot up and pinch the edges together.

3. Pop into the fridge for an hour (at least), so they can firm up before cooking them.

4. Preheat your grill and drop the heat to med–hot. Cook as for charcoal grill, only cover the patties.

5. Toast the buns (open face down) for the last minute or so of cooking.

6. Let the burgers stand for a few minutes to let the cheese cool a bit.

7. Serve in the buns with your favorite condiments and toppings.

Blue Vidalia Burgers

Vidalia may bring computer software to the minds of some, but to others, it is a particularly sweet kind of onion. For the purposes of this recipe, we'll stick with the edible onion version.

Serves: 8

Time: 30 min

Ingredients

Onion Parcel:

- 2 Large, Sweet (Vidalia) Onions, Cut into Thick Slices

- 1 Tbsp Butter

Patties:

- 2 lbs. Ground Beef
- ¾ Tsp Salt
- ¼ Tsp Black Pepper

The Rest:

- 1 cup (4 oz) Crumbled Blue Cheese
- 4 oz Cream Cheese
- 2 Tsp Worcestershire Sauce
- ½ Tsp Black Pepper
- ½ Tsp Dried Dill Weed – Leaves and Stems (Also known as dill)
- 8 Hamburger Buns, Cut Open (Toasted if You Like)

Directions

1. Bring your charcoal to medium heat or preheat your gas grill on full before dropping the setting to med–high. The gas grill will be covered during cooking.

2. Obtain a 36"x18" piece of heavy–duty foil and fold it in half to make a really strong, foil square. Pack the onions and

dots of butter in the center, bring the foil edges over and make a sealed parcel. Don't wrap them too tightly though.

3. Grill the package directly over the heat until the onions are just tender. Turn the foil package now and then (25–30 min).

4. While you wait for the onions to cook, mix up the meat and seasoning. Divide into 8 balls and pat them down until ¾″ thick.

5. Grill them on a lightly oiled rack until the internal temp is 160°F, turning once (14–18min)

6. Mix together: blue cheese, cream cheese, Worcestershire sauce, pepper, and dill. Lift the onions out of their foil bed (leave any juice behind) and toss to coat.

7. Spoon this mixture over the burgers in buns. Enjoy!

Conclusion

Congrats on completing all 30 delicious Picnic Recipes! We hope you enjoyed all 30 recipes and that they were easy to whip up and tasty.

So, what happens next?

Practice! That's right, the only way to get better at creating these delicious recipes is to practice. Be sure to keep cooking and enjoying all the delicious recipes featured in this Easy Picnic Cookbook. All of which will be easy to follow and can be created in a hassle-free environment. So, whenever you feel like you have mastered all the recipes in this book, grab another one of our books and let your culinary creativity run wild.

Remember, drop us a review if you loved what you read and until we meet again, keep on cooking delicious food.

Made in the
USA
Columbia, SC